Paleo Recipes for Rapid Weight Loss

50 Delicious, Quick & Easy Recipes to Help Melt Your Damn Stubborn Fat Away!

Copyright © 2015 by Fat Loss Nation

Disclaimer

This document is geared towards providing exact and reliable information in regards to the topic and issue covered. The publication is sold with the idea that the publisher is not required to render accounting, officially permitted, or otherwise, qualified services. If advice is necessary, legal or professional, a practiced individual in the profession should be ordered.

- From a Declaration of Principles which was accepted and approved equally by a Committee of the American Bar Association and a Committee of Publishers and Associations.

About This Book

This book aims to introduce you to the benefits of the popular Paleo Diet and give you 50 of the best paleo recipes for rapid weight loss. It's informational and to the point, and organized into sections on breakfast, lunch, supper, snacks and desserts so you won't be missing any meals! Each section is complete with the needed information.

You will find concluding remarks and a list of resources for additional recipes at the end of this book. I will also give you a preview of another book of mine which I am sure will delight you as well.

The following table of contents will show you exactly what is covered in this book.

Table of Contents

Introduction

In this age of processed and genetically modified foods, preservatives and artificial flavors, there's a growing movement toward eating a more natural and wholesome diet. One of the cutting-edge diets in this movement is the Paleo Diet, which was Google's most-searched-for method of weight loss in 2013.

The Paleo Diet, also known as the Caveman Diet or Stone Age Diet, is based upon the diet that humans ate for millions of years during the Paleolithic Stone Age prior to the introduction of agriculture. The idea behind the Paleo Diet, backed by more than thirty years of scientific research, is that our ancestors became evolutionarily adapted to the foods of the Paleolithic Age, and that many of the diseases and health issues that we've developed during the agricultural age have been brought on because of the changes in our diet stemming from the introduction of agricultural some 10,000 years ago.

The advent of agriculture initiated an irrevocable change in humanity's lifestyle and health. Our forefathers settled down and started farming, while also forming societies and towns. New foods like grains and flours appeared— foods our bodies weren't conditioned for. And other new foods have been appearing in large quantities in our modern world, like processed foods, artificial additives, sugars, trans-fats, complex carbohydrates and genetically modified foods. These new foods have led us to health problems like obesity, heart disease, diabetes and a host of chronic conditions that humanity never suffered from in the Stone Age.

Many people mistakenly believe that eating fatty foods leads to weight gain. That's somewhat true for bad fats like trans-fats, but not necessarily true for good fats, like those from nuts and organic meat. Good fats are only stored in your body when your body doesn't need the energy they provide. As soon as your body needs the energy from good fats, the fat cells release them into the bloodstream and provide that energy.

But bad fats are stubborn and are not released easily when your body needs energy: they lock up and consequently build up within your body. When this fat locks up, your body is deprived of the fat's energy, so your body signals you to eat so that you'll have the energy you need. Basically, your body is still hungry, even though you've just eaten, because the body can't use the junk food you've eaten. This naturally leads to obesity.

Eating a lot of sugar also leads to obesity. The sugar builds up in your bloodstream, becoming toxic. This leads your body to produce more insulin in order to combat this toxicity. Your body can't use all this sugar at once, so your body stores it. But the body has limited ability to store sugar and carbohydrates, so it converts the carbohydrates into fat—but unfortunately this fat is mostly stored instead of being used. So the fats build up and promote obesity.

A study conducted by the Department of Medicine at the University of California San Francisco School of Medicine found that, after test patients had consumed a Paleo Diet for ten days, their total cholesterol dropped by 16%, their LDP cholesterol by 22% and their triglycerides by 35%. Eight out of nine showed significantly improved blood circulation and lipid metabolism. The Paleo Diet was shown to improve glucose tolerance, decrease insulin secretion and increase insulin sensitivity.

The basic Paleo Diet consists of fruits, vegetables, greens, nuts, seeds, eggs, fish, fowl and meat. The meat should ideally come from grass-fed animals and should be free of artificial additives. Eggs should be from free-range chickens. The primary spices and condiments should be natural sea salt and plants that were once foraged, like turmeric, rosemary and garlic. Dark chocolate is acceptable, though you should limit or eliminate the sugar in it. Coffee and black tea are rich in antioxidants and are acceptable. The fats in nuts, seeds, avocados and healthy oils like coconut oil, olive oil, macadamia oil and avocado oil are fine.

You should steer clear of grains, flour from grains, pasta, legumes (including peanuts), dairy products, food additives, artificial sweeteners, carbonated drinks and highly processed foods. You should also avoid deep-fried foods. Foods that are high in carbohydrates tend to be fattening and should be limited.

This book offer fifty mouthwatering recipes, from basic recipes like Steak and Eggs to more elaborate ones like Italian Sausage Pizza and Double-layered Chocolate Cake. The recipes are all tried-and-true, and are presented in a clear, consistent and easy-to-follow format. They tell you at a glance the number of servings, prep time and cooking time, and they list the directions in numbered steps. The recipes are separated into five convenient chapters: Breakfast, Lunch, Supper, Snacks and Desserts.

You can easily incorporate these recipes into your lifestyle, no matter how busy your schedule might be. The recipes have been chosen for their ability to help you lose weight while enjoying a wide variety of nutritious and delicious foods. We've also tried to offer a wide variety of recipes, to give you some ideas of what you can eat on this diet. This might also help you modify some of your own non-Paleo recipes from other cookbooks to fit in with the Paleo Diet.

We hope this book leads you to appreciate the joys of the healthful and natural Paleo Diet.

Breakfast Recipes

A lot of nutritional experts rate breakfast as the most important meal of the day, and who am I to argue? Eating a satisfying and healthy meal definitely seems like a great way to start the day, especially if it tastes great. These breakfast recipes definitely qualify.

Note: The numbers after the recipes refer to our sources for the recipes. See the Helpful Resources section toward the end of the book.

Omelet Muffins (1)

Easy and hearty muffins, without using regular flour. They take only about 35 minutes to prepare, including the cooking time.

Servings: 8 muffins

Prep Time: 15 minutes

Cooking Time: 20 minutes

Ingredients

- 8 eggs
- 8 ounces cooked ham, crumbled
- 1 cup diced red bell pepper
- 1 cup diced onion
- ¼ teaspoon salt
- 1/8 teaspoon ground black pepper
- 2 tablespoons water

Directions

1. Preheat your oven to 350 F (175 C). Grease 8 muffin cups or use paper liners.

2. Beat the eggs in a large bowl. Mix all the other ingredients into the eggs, and pour the mix into the muffin cups.

3. Bake for 18 to 20 minutes, until muffins are set in the middle.

Pancakes with Pureed Strawberries (1)

These delicious pancakes are more dense than normal because they use almond meal instead of flour, so they're quite filling.

Servings: 10

Prep Time: 10 minutes

Cooking Time: 20 minutes

Ingredients

- 1 ½ cups almond meal
- 2 eggs
- ½ teaspoon vanilla extract
- ½ teaspoon ground cinnamon
- ½ cup applesauce
- ¼ teaspoon baking powder
- ¼ cup coconut milk, or more as needed
- 1 teaspoon olive oil, for frying
- 1 cup strawberries, for topping

Directions

1. In a medium-sized bowl, mix the almond meal, eggs, vanilla extract, cinnamon, baking powder and coconut milk.

2. Spread some of the olive oil over a griddle at medium-high heat. Spoon the batter onto the griddle and fry until bubbles form and the pancake's edges are dry. Flip the pancakes and cook until they're browned.

3. Repeat step 2 with the rest of the batter.

4. Puree the strawberries in a food processor or blender and top the pancakes with the pureed strawberries.

Baked Eggs with Asparagus and Leeks (2)

A good, quick way to get some fresh greens into your breakfast. For those who want to stay clear of bacon, you can substitute any breakfast meat for it.

Servings: 4

Prep Time: 5 minutes

Cooking Time: 15 minutes

Ingredients

- 4 eggs
- 1 leek, sliced
- 1 bunch asparagus
- 4 slices bacon
- 1 clove garlic, minced
- 3 tablespoons fresh chives, minced
- Sea salt and black pepper to taste

Directions

1. Preheat oven to 400 F.

2. Fry the bacon in an oven-friendly skillet over medium-high heat for about 3 minutes per side, until tender.

3. Add the garlic and leek and cook for another 2 or 3 minutes. You can optionally pour off some of the fat.

4. Add the asparagus and cook another 6 minutes or until soft and tender.

5. Add the eggs and seasoning and place the skillet in the oven for 3 or 4 minutes.

6. Garnish with fresh chives and serve.

Banana Walnut Muffins (3)

This terrific breakfast is sweetened with stevia, an all-natural product extracted from a plant. Who said healthy can't taste good?

Servings: 12

Prep Time: 10 minutes

Cooking Time: 20-25 minutes

Ingredients

- 3 eggs
- ¼ cup coconut oil
- 2 medium bananas
- 3 dates, pitted
- 10 drops stevia
- ¼ cup coconut flour
- ¼ teaspoon Celtic sea salt
- ½ teaspoon baking soda
- ½ cup walnuts, toasted and chopped

Directions

1. Preheat oven to 350 F.

2. Put the eggs, bananas, dates and stevia in a blender and blend at medium speed until combined.

3. Add coconut flour, salt and baking soda, blending until smooth.

4. Fold the walnuts in.

5. Scoop ¼ cup batter into a muffin pan that is either greased or lined.

6. Bake for 20-25 minutes, until they're browning and not soft to the touch.

Apple Cinnamon Muffins (4)

This versatile recipe allows for various substitutions. You can reduce the applesauce by ¼ cup and substitute an overripe banana before you blend. You can also add up to a half cup of chopped nuts, blueberries or raspberries. Another option is to add 3 tablespoons of cocoa powder.

Servings: 12

Prep Time: 10 minutes

Cooking Time: 15 minutes

Ingredients

- 5 eggs
- 1 cup applesauce
- ½ cup coconut flour
- 3 tablespoons cinnamon
- 1 teaspoon baking soda
- 1 teaspoon vanilla (optional)
- ¼ cup coconut oil
- 2 tablespoons honey (optional)

Directions

1. Preheat oven to 400 F.

2. Grease a muffin pan with a small amount of coconut oil.

3. Put all the ingredients into a medium-sized bowl. Blend or whisk until well-mixed.

4. Let the mix stand for 5 minutes.

5. Use a 1/3 cup measure to spoon the mix into the muffin tins.

6. Bake until the muffins start to brown and aren't soft when you lightly touch the top, normally 12-15 minutes.

7. Let muffins cool for 2 minutes. Optionally drizzle with honey.

8. Serve.

Weekend Warrior Omelet (5)

This breakfast is a real nutritional warrior, featuring a slate of nutrients that comes close to providing your entire day's requirement.

Servings: 2

Prep Time: 10 minutes

Cooking Time: 10 minutes

Ingredients

- 2 large free-range organic eggs, scrambled
- 1 teaspoon olive oil
- 2 green onions, diced
- 1 cup fresh organic spinach leaves
- 2 organic small tomatoes
- ½ fresh organic avocado, sliced into bite-sized pieces

Directions

1. Put olive oil in a non-stick omelet pan set on low heat. Add onions and sauté until tender.

2. Add eggs and cook on a low heat for about 2 minutes.

3. Stir in the remaining ingredients.

4. Fold and flip the omelet until the eggs are fully cooked.

Steak and Eggs (6)

This hearty breakfast really hits the spot. The vegetables and greens add complete nutrition, and this breakfast could easily serve as the main meal of the day.

Servings: Full breakfast for two

Prep Time: 10 minutes

Cooking Time: 20 minutes

Ingredients

- ½ pound boneless beef steak, sliced into quarter-inch pieces
- ¼ teaspoon freshly ground black pepper
- ¼ teaspoon sea salt (optional)
- 2 teaspoons coconut oil, lard, or tallow, divided
- ¼ yellow onion, diced
- 4 mushrooms, sliced
- 1 red bell pepper, diced
- 1 handful spinach or arugula
- 2 eggs

Directions

1. Season the sliced steak with salt and pepper.

2. Put a large sauté pan onto medium-high heat.

3. When the pan is hot, add 1 teaspoon coconut oil, onions, mushrooms and steak. Sauté until steak is slightly cooked.

4. Add bell pepper and spinach, and finish cooking the steak.

5. Meanwhile, put a small frying pan on medium heat and add the remaining coconut oil. Fry both eggs.

6. Divide the steak and vegetables onto two plates and top each with a fried egg. Serve.

Breakfast Hash (8)

This is a great way to use up leftovers, because you can add just about anything to this dish. Just shred or chop them up and throw them in.

Servings: 2

Prep Time: 10 minutes

Cooking Time: 15 minutes

Ingredients

- 1 tablespoon oil
- 1 minced garlic clove
- ½ chopped onion
- ½ sweet potato, grated
- 2 eggs
- ¼ teaspoon cayenne pepper
- Salt and pepper to taste

Directions

1. Heat pan to medium and add oil.

2. Lightly sauté the onion and potato.

3. Add spices to taste.

4. Stir the eggs in and cover.

5. Cook for 3 minutes.

Tropical Fruit Smoothie (11)

This smoothie is loaded with antioxidants, enzymes, minerals and vitamins, and packs a wallop. It just takes minutes to make, and you can drink it on the go.

Servings: 2 glasses

Prep Time: 10 minutes

Cooking Time: No cooking

Ingredients

- 1 cup frozen mango chunks
- 1 cup chopped pineapple
- 1 frozen banana, peeled and sliced
- 1 kiwi, peeled and sliced
- 1 cup orange juice
- ½ cup ice cubes

Directions

1. Combine all the ingredients in a blender until smooth.

2. If needed, you can add more ice to thicken it.

3. You can refrigerate part of this for up to two days.

Banana Nut Bread (11)

This recipe is easy to make and puts those extra bananas to good use.

Servings: 8

Prep Time: 15 minutes

Cooking Time: 60 minutes

Ingredients

- 1 cup ripe banana, mashed
- ¼ cup raw honey
- 3 large eggs, whisked
- ¼ cup coconut oil, melted
- 1 teaspoon vanilla extract
- 2 cups almond flour
- 1 teaspoon baking soda
- ½ teaspoon ground cinnamon
- Pinch of salt
- ½ cup chopped walnuts or pecans

Directions

1. Preheat your oven to 350 F. Grease a loaf pan.

2. In a large bowl, combine the banana, honey, eggs, coconut oil and vanilla extract.

3. Add the rest of the ingredients except the walnuts, and beat until smooth.

4. Fold the walnuts into the mixture.

5. Pour the batter into the greased loaf pan.

6. Bake until a knife inserted into the center comes out clean, approximately an hour.

7. Cool the bread in the pan for 15 minutes and then carefully turn it to take it out of the pan onto a wire rack to further cool.

Crustless Bacon Quiche (11)

This relatively quick quiche is easy to whip up because you don't have to make a crust for it.

Servings: 8

Prep Time: 15 minutes

Cooking Time: 50 minutes

Ingredients

- 1 pound bacon, raw
- 6 large eggs
- 1 medium onion, diced
- ½ cup unsweetened coconut milk

Directions

1. Preheat oven to 425 F.

2. Cook the bacon until crisp in a large skillet, draining it on a paper towel.

3. When cool, chop the bacon into pieces.

4. Put the bacon pieces and onions into a greased pie plate.

5. Beat the eggs and coconut milk together in a bowl, and then pour them into the pie plate and mix them with the bacon and onions.

6. Bake for 25 minutes and then reduce the temperature in the oven to 325 F. Cover the dish with foil and then bake for an extra 10-15 minutes until the center is set.

7. Remove the dish from the oven and let it sit, uncovered, for 5 minutes.

8. Slice as you serve it.

Lunch Recipes

Most of these lunch recipes can qualify as either a lunch in themselves or as a main course for supper. Most of them only take 10-15 minutes for initial prep time, and some of them don't require cooking. All but a couple of them take under an hour for combined prep and cooking time.

Salmon with Citrus Salad (6)

This is a deliciously filling but low-calorie lunch for two.

Servings: 2

Prep Time: 10 minutes

Cooking Time: 15-35 minutes

Ingredients

- ¾ pound fresh or frozen salmon filets
- ½ teaspoon sea salt
- ¼ teaspoon freshly ground black pepper
- ½ pound mixed greens (or use fresh pea shoots)
- 1 cup sugar snap peas, trimmed
- 1 radish, trimmed and thinly sliced
- 1/3 cup roasted sunflower seeds
- Juice of ½ orange
- Juice of ½ lemon (or use lemon segments)
- 1 tablespoon olive oil

Directions

1. Preheat oven to 425 F.

2. If using fresh salmon filets, season both sides with salt and pepper. If using frozen filets, season after the filets have been cooking for a few minutes so the seasoning will stick to the filet.

3. Put the filets on a broiler pan (or you can use a wire rack over a baking sheet) and put the pan in the oven. Bake until the salmon flakes easily with a fork and the internal temperature of the salmon reaches 145 F. For fresh salmon, this will take 15-18 minutes, and for frozen, 30-35 minutes.

4. Meanwhile, combine the rest of the ingredients in a large mixing bowl, tossing it to coat, and then season the salad.

Cantaloupe and Avocado Salad (6)

Though this seems like an odd combination of ingredients, it really tastes great. The honey adds a lot of sweetness, so if you don't like a sweet salad, you can cut back on the honey.

Servings: 4

Prep Time: 15 minutes

Cooking Time: No cooking

Ingredients

- 3 tablespoons fresh lime juice
- 4 teaspoons raw honey
- 2 tablespoons olive oil
- ½ teaspoon sea salt
- 1 cantaloupe (3 pounds), quartered and seeded
- 1 avocado
- 1 cup cherry or grape tomatoes, halved

Directions

1. Whisk the lime juice, honey, oil and sea salt together in a large bowl.

2. Cut the cantaloupe quarters in half lengthwise and peel the skin off them with a knife. Slice the wedges lengthwise into half-inch pieces.

3. Cut the avocado lengthwise into quarters and then into half-inch slices.

4. Add the rest of the ingredients to the large bowl and toss the salad to coat.

Indian Coleslaw (6)

You can add a lean protein if you want to turn this dish into a complete and filling lunch for two. This salad will keep fine for two or three days in the fridge.

Servings: 4

Prep Time: 20 minutes

Cooking Time: No cooking

Ingredients

- 1 small green cabbage, finely chopped (about 3 cups)
- 3 medium tomatoes, diced
- 1 cup unsweetened shredded coconut
- ½ cup almond flour
- 1 large date, soaked, pitted and mashed
- Juice of 1 lemon
- 2 tablespoons olive oil
- ½ teaspoon ground brown mustard seed
- ½ teaspoon ground cumin seed
- ¼ teaspoon turmeric
- 1 tablespoon jalapeno, minced (optional)
- Sea salt to taste (optional)

Directions

1. In a large salad bowl, toss the cabbage, tomatoes, coconut and almond flour.

2. Put the soaked date in a small bowl and mash it. Add the rest of the ingredients (listed below the soaked date)

to the small bowl and whisk them together until they've formed a smooth dressing.

3. Pour this dressing into the large bowl and combine it completely with the cabbage, tomatoes, coconut and almond flour.

Spicy Tuna Salad (6)

This makes a light lunch for two people. You can optionally serve it on top of lettuce or mixed greens.

Servings: 2

Prep Time: 15 minutes

Cooking Time: No cooking

Ingredients

- 2 cans tuna (oil-packed recommended)
- 20 (about 1 cup) green or black olives, chopped
- 2 green onions, chopped
- 1 jalapeno pepper, finely chopped (no seeds and/or less jalapeno if you want less spice)
- 3 tablespoons capers, rinsed
- ½ teaspoon red chili flakes
- Juice of 2 lemons
- Splash of olive oil
- 1 head butter lettuce or mixed greens (optional)
- 1 avocado, sliced

Directions

1. Combine all the ingredients, with sliced avocado on top.

2. You can serve it at once or store it in the fridge for a day, which increases the flavor. But in either case, add the avocado just before you serve the salad.

Turkey Vegetable Meatballs (6)

These meatballs go well with eggs for breakfast, as well as for the normal uses for meatballs. For meatballs that are a little juicier, you can add a half cup of chopped mushrooms to the recipe.

Servings: 4

Prep Time: 15 minutes

Cooking Time: 25 minutes

Ingredients

- 2 medium carrots (or a handful of baby carrots)
- 1 red or green bell pepper
- 5 large mushrooms
- Handful of fresh parsley
- ½ yellow onion
- 1 clove garlic
- 2 tsp granulated garlic (garlic salt)
- 2 tablespoons Italian seasoning
- ½ teaspoon freshly ground black pepper
- 1 pound ground turkey or chicken

Directions

1. Preheat your oven to 350 F.

2. Put everything except the ground turkey into a food processor and blend until well-chopped.

3. Put the contents of the food processor into a large bowl. Add the ground turkey and mix thoroughly.

4. Form meatballs and put them onto an ungreased baking sheet.

5. Bake for about 25 minutes.

Chicken Stew (7)

You can add additional vegetables or spices to this versatile recipe.

Servings: 4

Prep Time: 10 minutes

Cooking Time: 60 minutes

Ingredients

- 2 boneless chicken breast halves, skinned and cut into cubes
- 2 sweet potatoes, peeled and chopped into cubes
- ½ cup chicken broth
- 2 red onions, chopped
- 2 teaspoons olive oil
- 2 cloves garlic, minced
- 1 bunch spinach, chopped
- Paprika, red pepper and sea salt to taste

Directions

1. Put large sauté pan (with cover) on medium heat, adding olive oil when it gets hot.

2. Sauté the onion and garlic until they're soft.

3. Add the remaining ingredients, adding the chicken broth last to make a stew-like consistency.

4. When the broth starts to boil, lower the heat to medium-low, cover the pan and cook until the chicken is no longer pink and the sweet potatoes are soft.

Walnut Banana Bread (8)

One minor inconvenience of the Paleo Diet is that it's hard to find flourless bread to buy. But with this recipe, it's a snap to throw the ingredients into a blender, then set the mix in a pan and pop it into the oven. You can substitute almond flour in place of the coconut flour and/or the walnuts.

Servings: 12

Prep Time: 10 minutes

Cooking Time: 60 minutes

Ingredients

- ¼ cup oil
- 1 tablespoon honey
- 1 tablespoon vanilla essence
- 3 eggs
- 3 medium bananas
- 1 teaspoon baking soda
- ¼ teaspoon salt
- 1 ½ cups ground walnuts
- ¼ cup coconut flour

Directions

1. Preheat your oven to 350 F.

2. Grease an 8 x 4-inch loaf pan.

3. Blend the oil, honey, vanilla, eggs and bananas in a food processor.

4. Blend in the other ingredients and pour into a prepared pan.

5. Bake for about an hour.

6. Leave it out to cool before turning out and slicing.

Broccoli Beef Soup (8)

This is a quick and easy way to a delicious and filling lunch or supper.

Servings: 6

Prep Time: 10 minutes

Cooking Time: 15 minutes

Ingredients

- 3 pints beef broth
- 1 pound chopped broccoli
- 1 pound diced cooked beef
- 1 minced garlic clove
- ½ minced onion
- 4 tablespoons soy sauce
- 4 tablespoons grated fresh ginger

Directions

1. In a large pot, heat the broth to a simmer.

2. Stir in all the other ingredients.

3. Simmer until broccoli is tender.

4. Serve with mashed potatoes.

Bison Patties (8)

Bison sales reached nearly a quarter million dollars in 2012. More and more people are discovering this healthy meat, which is leaner than lean beef but tastes about the same.

Servings: 4

Prep Time: 10 minutes

Cooking Time: 20 minutes

Ingredients

- Pepper and salt to taste
- 2 minced garlic cloves
- 1 egg
- 1 jalapeno pepper
- 1 tablespoon chopped fresh rosemary
- 1 teaspoon chopped fresh thyme
- 1 minced onion
- 1 pound minced bison

Directions

1. Mix all the ingredients in a bowl, and form into patties.

2. Fry in a skillet over medium-high heat until cooked through, cooking both sides.

3. Serve hot.

Cashew Date Mint Smoothie (9)

Smoothies make terrific meal replacements; they're quick and easy to make, and are loaded with nutrition. Mint triggers a feeling of fullness, so it serves as an appetite suppressant.

Servings: 2

Prep Time: 10 minutes

Cooking Time: No cooking

Ingredients

- 1½ cups distilled water
- 1 cup chopped spinach leaves
- 10 pieces mint leaves
- 2 whole pitted dates
- 2 tablespoons raw cashew butter

Directions

1. Thoroughly wash the mint and spinach leaves.

2. Blend the mint and spinach in a blender until smooth.

3. Add the rest of the ingredients and blend them until smooth.

4. Serve.

Turkey Avocado Roll-up (11)

Fast and portable lunch for two people on the go.

Servings: 4 small roll-ups

Prep Time: 15 minutes

Cooking Time: No cooking

Ingredients

- 8 large leaves Romaine lettuce
- 5 ounces deli turkey, chopped
- 1 ripe avocado, pitted and chopped
- ¼ cup minced red onion
- 1 stalk celery, minced
- 1 medium carrot, shredded
- 1 tablespoon Tahini sauce
- 1 teaspoon fresh lemon juice
- Salt and pepper to taste

Directions

1. Lay four lettuce leaves out flat and set the other four beside them.

2. Put the rest of the vegetable and the turkey in a bowl and toss them.

3. Season with the Tahini sauce, lemon juice and salt, mixing them in.

4. Spoon the mixture onto the middle of each of the flattened lettuce leaves.

5. Top each of these leaves with another leaf and roll them up.

Lemongrass Scallop Soup (11)

Chances are, you've never had soup like this; but once you've tried it, it will be a mainstay.

Servings: 4-6

Prep Time: 15 minutes

Cooking Time: 20 minutes

Ingredients

- 1 pound bay scallops, raw
- 2 tablespoons coconut oil, divided
- 2 red bell peppers, chopped
- 2 green onions, chopped
- 1 cup sliced mushrooms
- 1 tablespoon red curry paste
- 1 teaspoon chopped lemongrass
- 1 cup unsweetened coconut milk
- 4 cups organic chicken stock
- ¼ cup fresh chopped cilantro
- 2 tablespoons fresh lime juice
- 2 tablespoons fish sauce
- 1 cup fresh arugula leaves
- 1 tablespoon fresh lemon zest

Directions

1. Put a stockpot on medium heat and put a tablespoon of coconut oil in it.

2. Add the scallops, frying for about 30 seconds on each side, until each side is lightly browned.

3. Take the scallops out of the stockpot.

4. Put the other tablespoon of coconut oil into the stockpot and stir in the bell pepper, green onion and sliced mushrooms.

5. Add the red curry paste, lemongrass and chicken stock, stirring.

6. Bring to a boil and then reduce heat, simmering for ten minutes.

7. Stir in the rest of the ingredients except the arugula and lemon zest. Simmer for about 5 minutes, until the scallops are cooked through.

8. Garnish with the arugula and lemon zest.

Supper Recipes

Low-calorie foods aren't necessarily the end-all for losing weight. If your supper isn't sufficiently filling, you're more liable to snack later in the evening. These recipes were chosen for their ability to fill you up without producing an excess of calories. They're also chosen for their great taste; after all, what good is a recipe no one wants to eat?

Paleo Chili (1)

Though this chili is made without beans in order to satisfy paleo standards, this smoky dish has garnered rave reviews even from non-paleo diners. You can add a 15-ounce can of drained and rinsed pinto beans if you want, and you can substitute bison or turkey sausage for the pork sausage.

Servings: 2

Prep Time: 15 min

Cooking Time: 35 min

Ingredients

- 1 dried chipotle pepper, stem removed
- 1 cup boiling water
- 1 ½ teaspoons coconut oil
- 1 cup chopped yellow onion
- 1 cup chopped green bell pepper
- 1 cup chopped red bell pepper
- 4 garlic cloves, minced
- 1 pound ground bison
- ½ pound spicy ground pork sausage

- 1 tablespoon chili powder
- 1 tablespoon ground cumin
- 1 teaspoon dried oregano
- 1 teaspoon unsweetened cocoa powder
- 1 teaspoon Worcestershire sauce
- 1 (28-ounce) can crushed tomatoes
- 1 ½ teaspoons kosher salt
- ½ teaspoon ground black pepper

Directions

1. Soak the chipotle pepper in the boiling water for about 10 minutes, until softened. Remove the pepper from the water and mince it.

2. In a large pot, melt the coconut oil over medium heat. Cook and stir the onion and the red and green bell pepper for 5 to 10 minutes, until tender. Add the garlic and the minced chipotle, stirring it into this mix, and cook for about a minute, until it's fragrant.

3. Add the bison and sausage to the mix, cooking and stirring for 10 to 12 minutes, until it's browned and crumbly.

4. Stir the chili powder, cumin, cocoa powder, oregano and Worcestershire sauce into the mix, and then add the rest of the ingredients. Bring everything to a boil, then reduce to a low heat and simmer for about 10 minutes, until the flavors are blended.

Meat Loaf (6)

This delicious and filling dish offers complete nutrition.

Servings: Dinner for two people, with leftovers for lunch

Prep Time: 15 minutes

Cooking Time: 75-85 minutes

Ingredients

- ¼ teaspoon dried sage
- 1 teaspoon sea salt (optional)
- 1 teaspoon dry mustard
- ½ teaspoon fresh ground pepper
- 1 teaspoon granulated garlic
- 1 teaspoon chipotle chili powder
- 4 cloves garlic, minced
- 1 small yellow onion, finely chopped
- 1 cup red cabbage chopped
- 2 tablespoons coconut milk (canned, full fat)
- ½ teaspoon hot pepper sauce
- 1/3 cup almond meal
- 1 egg, beaten
- 1 ½ pounds lean ground beef
- ½ cup unsweetened barbecue sauce (optional)

Directions

1. Preheat the oven to 350 F.

2. In a large bowl, combine everything except the BBQ sauce and ground beef. Mix well.

3. Add ground beef to mix, combining with a fork.

4. Either put this mixture into an ungreased loaf pan or shape the mixture into a loaf and put on an ungreased baking pan.

5. Pour the BBQ sauce onto the top of the meatloaf.

6. Bake, uncovered, until an internal meatloaf temperature of 160 F is reached (or until there isn't any pink color left in the center of the loaf). This should take 75-85 minutes.

7. Take the loaf out of the oven and let it stand for 5 minutes. Slice and serve.

Baked Salmon with Rosemary and Pecans (6)

This is a quick and tasty dinner that goes well with any salad.

Servings: Dinner for 2

Prep Time: 10 minutes

Cooking Time: 12-15 minutes

Ingredients

- Coconut oil for greasing pan
- ¾ pound salmon filet, skin left on
- 2 tablespoons pecans, chopped
- 1 tablespoon rosemary, chopped
- ¼ teaspoon sea salt (optional)

Directions

1. Preheat oven to 350 F.

2. Lightly grease a baking pan.

3. Put the salmon in the pan with the skin side down.

4. Sprinkle the other ingredients onto to fish.

5. Bake until the salmon flakes lightly with a fork, 12-15 minutes.

Pork Loin with Peppers, Mushrooms and Onions (6)

This meal tastes absolutely gourmet, even though it brings out the cave dweller in you.

Servings: Dinner for 2, with leftovers for lunch

Prep Time: 10 minutes

Cooking Time: 25 minutes

Ingredients

- 1 tablespoon coconut oil
- 1 pound pork loin
- 1 tablespoon caraway seeds
- ½ teaspoon sea salt
- ¼ teaspoon freshly ground black pepper
- 1 red onion
- 3 porcini mushrooms, sliced
- 2 red bell peppers, sliced
- 4 cloves garlic, minced
- ¼ cup chicken broth

Directions

1. Wash and chop the vegetables.

2. Thinly slice the pork loin. Season the pork with caraway seeds, salt and black pepper.

3. Heat a large pan (with lid) over medium-high heat, adding coconut oil when pan gets hot.

4. Add the pork loin, browning it slightly.

5. Add the onions and mushrooms, sautéing until the mushrooms are brown and the onions slightly translucent.

6. Add the peppers and chicken broth, cover and simmer until the vegetables become tender and the pork is completely cooked.

Japanese Ratatouille (8)

This quick vegetable dish is great by itself, or you can serve it with your favorite meat. You can add chopped sausage or salami to the recipe for a complete meal. You can substitute rosemary for the oregano and basil.

Servings: 4

Prep Time: 10 minutes

Cooking Time: 10 minutes

Ingredients

- 1 tablespoon chopped fresh oregano
- 1 tablespoon chopped fresh basil
- ¼ teaspoon cayenne pepper
- Pepper and salt to taste
- ¼ cup cooking oil
- 2 Japanese eggplants
- 6 tomatoes
- 2 bell peppers
- 4 minced garlic cloves
- 1 minced onion
- 2 zucchinis

Directions

1. Peel and chop the eggplant thinly, then put it in a colander and sprinkle with salt. Let it sit for twenty minutes.

2. Meanwhile, dice the tomatoes, bell peppers, garlic, onions and zucchinis.

3. Heat oil in soup pot.

4. Sauté the garlic and onion for 1 minute.

5. Stir in the remaining vegetable and sauté for 1 minute.

6. Stir in the remaining ingredients and simmer until the eggplant is soft, 5-8 minutes.

Crockpot Lean Beef Stew (8)

There's nothing like the long, slow crockpot process to draw out the inner flavors of foods.

Servings: 6

Prep Time: 10 minutes

Cooking Time: 2 ½ to 3 hours

Ingredients

- 1 tablespoon oil for sautéing
- 1 pound chopped lean beef
- 2 chopped onions
- 2 cloves garlic, minced
- 2 chopped bell peppers
- ½ teaspoon paprika
- ½ teaspoon cumin
- 1 teaspoon fresh chopped thyme
- 1 teaspoon fresh chopped rosemary
- 1 teaspoon fresh chopped sage
- 1 ½ pints beef stock
- 1 pint diced tomatoes
- Pepper and salt to taste

Directions

1. Heat oil in soup pot and stir the spices and herbs in.

2. Brown the beef and then remove it.

3. Sauté the onions and garlic.

4. Add the bell peppers and sauté briefly.

5. Stir in the browned beef and remaining ingredients.

6. Transfer to crock pot and cook for 2 to 2 ½ hours, until the beef is tender.

Italian Sausage Pizza (8)

I can't just dial up a delivery Paleo pizza, but this recipe is as tasty as any pizza you can buy, if not tastier.

Servings: 8

Prep Time: 15 minutes

Cooking Time: 45 minutes

Ingredients

- 2 eggs
- 3 tablespoons almond butter
- 1 cup almond flour
- ¼ teaspoon salt
- 1 tablespoon olive oil
- 1 Italian sausage, sliced
- 4 ounces mushrooms, chopped
- ½ onion, chopped
- 1 bell pepper, chopped
- ½ clove garlic, minced
- ½ cup marinara
- Fennel seed
- Oregano
- ½ cup cherry tomato halves

Directions

1. Preheat oven to 350 F.

2. Grease a baking tray.

3. Mix the eggs, almond butter, almond flour and salt together in a medium-sized bowl.

4. Knead the mix into a dough and press it flat. Carefully set the dough onto the prepared tray. Bake 10 minutes.

5. Meanwhile, heat the oil in a sauté pan over medium heat and lightly sauté the sausage, mushrooms and onion.

6. Add the bell pepper and garlic, and sauté 1 more minute.

7. Spread the marinara over the crust.

8. Sprinkle the sautéed vegetables and sausage over the crust.

9. Sprinkle the fennel seed and garlic over the vegetables and sausage.

10. Bake for 25 minutes.

11. Top with cherry tomatoes.

Grilled Turkey Cutlets with Tomato Salsa (11)

The tomato and cilantro flavor bursts from this quick and easy dish.

Servings: 4-6

Prep Time: 10 minutes

Cooking Time: 10 minutes

Ingredients

- 1 ½ pounds boneless turkey cutlets
- 1 tablespoon olive oil
- Salt and pepper to taste
- 2 ripe stem tomatoes, diced
- ½ small green pepper, diced
- ¼ cup diced red onion
- ½ cup chopped fresh cilantro
- 1 tablespoon fresh lime juice
- ½ teaspoon ground cumin

Directions

1. Preheat the grill to high.

2. Brush the turkey cutlets with olive oil. Season them with salt and pepper to taste.

3. Reduce the grill to medium-high. Grill the turkey for 4-6 minutes per side until they're cooked through.

4. Combine the rest of the ingredients in a small bowl. Serve them with the turkey.

Balsamic Roasted Chicken Legs (11)

This is an easy recipe and takes little prep time.

Servings: 4-6

Prep Time: 10 minutes

Cooking Time: 40-45 minutes

Ingredients

- 2 pounds raw chicken legs
- 2 tablespoons balsamic vinegar
- 2 tablespoons olive oil
- 1 teaspoon onion powder
- Salt and pepper to taste

Directions

1. Preheat your oven to 375 F. Grease a baking dish lightly.

2. Cut out any excess fat from the chicken legs. Sprinkle salt and pepper on the legs to taste, and put the chicken in the baking dish.

3. In a bowl, whisk together all the rest of the ingredients and drizzle it on the chicken.

4. Roast the chicken until it's cooked through, about 40-45 minutes.

5. Serve hot.

Beef and Mushroom Stroganoff (11)

This quick stroganoff dish makes for a hearty and satisfying meal.

Servings: 4-6

Prep Time: 15 minutes

Cooking Time: 30 minutes

Ingredients

- 1 ½ lbs. beef stew meat
- 2 tbsp. coconut oil
- 1 tbsp. minced garlic
- 1 large yellow onion, chopped
- 8 oz. sliced mushrooms
- 1 cup organic beef stock
- 1 cup unsweetened coconut milk
- Salt and pepper to taste

Directions

1. Apply salt and pepper to beef.

2. Heat a heavy skillet over medium heat and pour the coconut oil in.

3. Add the garlic and cook for 1 minute.

4. Stir the beef into the skillet and cook for 3-5 minutes, until evenly browned.

5. Stir the onion and mushrooms in well.

6. In a bowl, whisk the beef stock and coconut together and then add to the skillet, stirring well.

7. Bring to a boil and then reduce the heat. Simmer for 20 minutes.

8. Serve hot.

Lemon Roasted Pork Loin (11)

This delicious dish is easy to make.

Servings: 8

Prep Time: 30 minutes

Cooking Time: 60 minutes

Ingredients

- 2 pounds boneless pork loin
- 2 cloves garlic, minced
- 2 tablespoons fresh lemon zest
- 1 tablespoon fresh ground pepper
- ½ tablespoon coarse salt

Directions

1. Preheat the oven to 350 F.

2. Combine the garlic, lemon zest, pepper and salt in a small bowl. Rub the mixture onto the pork loin.

3. Put the loin into a roasting pan, baking for one hour, basting with the juices every 20 minutes. Bake until the internal temperature reaches 145 F.

4. Take the pork out and let it sit for 15 minutes before carving.

5. Serve hot.

Snack Recipes

Ideally, we like to stick to three square meals a day on the Paleo diet; but sometimes you get hungry between meals, and it's all-too-easy to fall prey to junk food snacks at these times. So it's probably a good idea to have healthy snacks available to prevent you from falling off the wagon.

Baked Sweet Potato Sticks (1)

You can use this dish as a snack or as part of a lunch. You can substitute whatever seasonings you like for the paprika, such as garlic salt, onion powder, salt or pepper.

Servings: 8

Prep Time: 15 minutes

Cooking Time: 50 minutes

Ingredients

- 1 tablespoon olive oil
- ½ teaspoon paprika
- 8 sweet potatoes, sliced lengthwise into quarters

Directions

1. Preheat the oven to 350 F. Lightly grease a baking sheet or spread aluminum foil over it.

2. Mix the olive oil and paprika in a large bowl. Add the sweet potato sticks, stirring them in order to coat them with the oil and paprika.

3. Bake for 50 minutes.

Baked Apple Chips (2)

This is an easy-to-make snack that you can store in a sealed container in the fridge. Instead of using an oven for this, you can use a food dehydrator.

Servings: 4

Prep Time: 5 minutes

Cooking Time: 90-120 minutes

Ingredients

- 3 apples
- Ground cinnamon, to taste

Directions

1. Preheat oven to 220 F.

2. Line 2 baking sheets with parchment paper.

3. Slice the apples thinly.

4. Spread out the apple slices on the paper, making sure none of them touch each other.

5. Sprinkle cinnamon on top of them and set sheets in the oven.

6. Leave the apples in the oven for an hour, and then flip the slices and cook for another hour.

7. Set the sheets on a cooling rack until cool.

8. Serve.

Deviled Eggs (3)

These tasty deviled eggs are naturally gluten-free and high in protein.

Servings: 10

Prep Time: 15 minutes

Cooking Time: None

Ingredients

- 5 large hard-boiled eggs, cooled and shelled
- 1 tablespoon mayonnaise or grape seed oil vegenaise
- 1 tablespoon Dijon mustard
- ¼ cup minced parsley
- ¼ cup finely diced celery
- 1 teaspoon minced shallots
- ¼ teaspoon pepper
- Paprika for garnish

Directions

1. Cut eggs in half. Remove yolks.

2. Put the yolks into a bowl and mash them.

3. Add the mayonnaise, mustard, parsley, celery, shallots, salt and pepper and mix them with the yolks.

4. Spoon the filling evenly into the egg whites.

5. Refrigerate until ready to serve.

6. Sprinkle paprika onto each deviled egg and serve.

Goji Power Bars (3)

These gluten-free power bars are great for recharging after a workout. Goji berries are considered by many to be a superfood. To make them softer, juicier and easier to digest, you can soak them. The best way is to put them in a bowl, spreading them out evenly, and then pour just enough boiling water in the bowl to cover them. Then let them soak for 10-15 minutes.

Servings: 16 2-inch square bars

Prep Time: 15 minutes

Cooking Time: 15 minutes

Ingredients

- 1 cup blanched almond flour
- 1 tablespoon coconut flour
- 2 tablespoons golden flax meal
- ¼ teaspoon Celtic sea salt
- ½ teaspoon baking soda
- 2 eggs
- ½ cup goji berries, soaked in ¼ cup boiling water to plump
- ½ cup raisins

Directions

1. Preheat oven to 350 F.

2. Combine the nut flours, flax meal, salt and baking soda.

3. Blend in the eggs with a hand blender.

4. Mix in the gojis and raisins with a large spoon.

5. Spread the mix into an 8 x 8-inch baking dish.

6. Bake for 15 minutes.

7. Cut into squares and serve.

Applesauce (5)

Here's a quick and easy recipe for delicious applesauce that is great for either a snack or for lunch.

Servings: 2

Prep Time: 5 minutes

Cooking Time: No cooking

- *Ingredients*
- ½ cup raw hazelnuts
- 2 tablespoons coconut milk
- 1 cored apple
- 4-6 grapes

Directions

1. Put the hazelnuts, milk and apple into a food processor. Blend on high for 10 seconds.

2. Add the grapes and pulse 5 times.

3. Serve.

Sautéed Shrimp (6)

This is a great treat for special occasions.

Servings: 2

Prep Time: 5 minutes

Cooking Time: 5 minutes

Ingredients

- 2 tablespoons olive or coconut oil
- ½ pound raw shrimp; deveined and peeled
- 2 tablespoons chili powder
- 1 tablespoon garlic powder
- ½ tablespoon parsley
- Cayenne pepper, to taste
- Freshly ground black pepper, to taste

Directions

1. Set a pan on medium-high heat, adding the oil to it.

2. Add shrimp when the pan is hot, and cook for one minute.

3. Stir in the rest of the ingredients and sauté for 3-5 more minutes, until the shrimp are pink.

Strawberry Roll-ups (6)

With this recipe, you make a sheet of dried fruit and then cut it into strips that you can roll up. You can spread whatever you want on the strips and then roll them up. Being dried, they keep for a long time, and you can take them along with you for a quick pick-me-up wherever you go. If you don't have a dehydrator, you can set the oven between 100 and 150 F and keep the door cracked open to facilitate air movement.

Servings: 6 roll-ups

Prep Time: 10 minutes

Cooking Time: 10-14 hours to dry.

Ingredients

- 2 large apples, cored and diced
- 2 cups strawberries, greens removed
- 1 teaspoon cinnamon
- ¼ cup purified water

Directions

1. Put all the ingredients into a blender and process for about 30 seconds, until smooth.

2. Pour the mixture onto a Teflon® or other PTFE sheet and put into a food dehydrator. If you don't have a PTFE sheet, don't use waxed paper or aluminum foil for this, but you can use plastic wrap or parchment paper.

3. Dehydrate for 6-8 hours and then flip the fruit and dry for another 4-6 hours. Don't over-dry them, or you won't be able to roll them up.

4. Cut into strips with a pizza cutter.

Dessert Recipes

Desserts aren't necessarily encouraged by some proponents of the Paleo Diet, because sweets tend to put weight on, not take it off. But it's important to remember that if you aren't enjoying your diet, your chances of staying on it for an extended period are diminished. And sometimes, in order to gain support for the Paleo Diet among your family members, you might need to dangle a carrot (cake) in front of them.

Zucchini Brownies (2)

People think I'm nuts when I tell them I put zucchini in my brownies. Well, I guess I am, because I also put nut butter in them. This recipe is a yummy way to use up some of the zucchini your neighbor gave you.

Servings: 4

Prep Time: 15 minutes

Cooking Time: 45 minutes

Ingredients

- 2 cups shredded zucchini
- 1 cup almond butter
- 1 ½ cups dark chocolate chips
- 1 egg
- 1/3 cup raw honey
- ¼ cup applesauce
- 2 teaspoons vanilla extract
- 3 tablespoons cocoa powder
- 1 teaspoon baking powder

Directions

1. Preheat oven to 350 F.

2. Combine all the ingredients in a food processor and process them.

3. Pour the mixture into a baking pan that has been greased or lined with parchment paper.

4. Bake for 45 minutes.

5. Don't cut the brownies until they're cool.

Almond Apple Cake (6)

This makes one cake or about a dozen muffins.

Servings: 12

Prep Time: 20 minutes

Cooking Time: 15-30 minutes

Ingredients

- 2 cups almond flour
- ½ teaspoon sea salt
- ½ teaspoon baking soda
- ¼ cup arrowroot powder (available online and at some farmer's markets)
- 1 teaspoon cinnamon
- ¼ cup coconut oil, melted
- ½ cup raw honey
- 1 egg
- 1 medium apple, peeled, cored and diced
- 1 tablespoon vanilla extract (optional)
- Dash freshly grated nutmeg

Directions

1. Preheat oven to 350 F.

2. Combine flour, salt, baking soda, arrowroot powder and cinnamon in a large bowl. Stir them well, to incorporate.

3. In a smaller bowl, combine the oil, honey, egg and vanilla extract, stirring to combine them.

4. Pour the wet ingredients into the large bowl, stirring to just barely combine them with the dry ingredients.

5. Add the apples and barely stir them in.

6. Pour the batter into a greased pan (or greased muffin pan) and sprinkle it with the nutmeg.

7. For a cake, bake for 30 minutes. For muffins, bake 14 minutes.

Chocolate Chip Cookies (6)

Hard to believe that dark chocolate chips are acceptable on a Paleo diet, but let's not look a gift horse in the mouth. Yum!

Servings: 24-36 cookies

Prep Time: 30 minutes

Cooking Time: 8-10 minutes

Ingredients

- 3 cups almond flour
- 1 teaspoon baking soda
- 1 teaspoon sea salt
- ½ cup coconut oil, melted
- ½ cup raw honey
- 2 large eggs
- 1 teaspoon vanilla extract
- 1 ½ cups dark chocolate chips

Directions

1. Preheat oven to 375 F.

2. Use parchment paper to line a baking sheet.

3. Combine the flour, salt and baking soda in a large mixing bowl.

4. In a medium-sized bowl, beat the eggs, honey and vanilla extract with a whisk or a hand mixer.

5. Slowly pour the wet ingredients into the bowl of dry ingredients, beating with a mixer or fork until combined.

6. Add the melted coconut oil. Blend until combined.

7. Stir in the chocolate chips.

8. Drop tablespoon-sized balls of the dough onto the baking sheet.

9. Bake for 8-10 minutes.

Almond Macaroons (6)

These macaroons are nice and lemony, so folks who aren't lemon fans might want to cut back on the lemon zest or the lemon juice. You can also substitute vanilla for the lemon juice and lemon zest.

Servings: 15-20 macaroons

Prep Time: 15 minutes

Cooking Time: 30 minutes

Ingredients

- 1 ¼ cups almonds, coarsely ground
- 1/8 teaspoon ground cinnamon
- 1 teaspoon lemon zest
- 2 egg whites, beaten
- ¼ cup raw honey
- 1 teaspoon lemon juice

Directions

1. Preheat oven to 250 F.

2. Line a baking sheet with parchment paper.

3. Grind or process the almonds into coarse flour, but don't reduce to paste. Set aside.

4. In a medium-sized bowl, mix the cinnamon and lemon zest.

5. Beat egg whites and add them to the bowl.

6. Add the lemon juice and honey and thoroughly stir them into the mix.

7. Add the almonds and blend them in.

8. Scoop the batter onto the parchment paper with a teaspoon, leaving sufficient space between spoonfuls.

9. Bake for 30 minutes.

10. Use a spatula to remove the macaroons while they're still a little warm.

Vanilla Pound Cake (6)

This is a rich, flavorful cake that's bound to please the whole family.

Servings: 12

Prep Time: 10 minutes

Cooking Time: 35-40 minutes

Ingredients

- 2 cups almond flour
- ½ cup coconut flour
- ¼ teaspoon salt
- 1 teaspoon baking soda
- 4 eggs
- 2/3 cup maple syrup or honey
- 2/3 cup solid coconut oil
- ½ cup plus 3 tablespoons coconut milk (full fat from a can)
- 2 tablespoons pure vanilla extract

Directions

1. Preheat your oven to 350 F. Grease a 9 x 5-inch loaf pan.

2. In a large bowl, combine the almond flour, coconut flour, salt and baking soda. Sift.

3. Put the eggs in a separate bowl and beat them lightly. Add the liquid ingredients and beat them lightly.

4. Add all the liquid ingredients to the dry ingredients and combine them, being careful not to over-mix.

5. Pour the batter into the greased loaf pan and bake for 35-40 minutes. A toothpick should come out cleanly when it's inserted into the center of the cake.

Double-Layered Chocolate Cake (10)

This is a spongy, moist, 9-inch, double-layer cake.

Servings: 12

Prep Time: 10 minutes

Cooking Time: 30-35 minutes

Cake Ingredients

- 1 ½ cup almond flour
- ½ cup coconut flour
- ½ teaspoon baking soda
- 6 tablespoons cacao powder or cocoa powder
- 1 cup full-fat coconut milk
- ¼ cup coconut oil
- ¼ cup honey
- ¼ cup coconut butter
- 2 eggs
- 2 teaspoons Vanilla

Frosting Ingredients

- 2 cups solid coconut oil (not melted)
- 1 cup honey
- 1 cup cocoa powder
- 2 tablespoons coconut milk

Directions

1. Preheat oven to 350 ° F.

2. Coat two 9" baking pans with coconut oil and line them with parchment circles.

3. In a large bowl, mix the almond flour, coconut flour, baking soda, and cacao powder, combining them well

4. In a separate bowl, mix the coconut milk, coconut oil, honey, coconut butter, eggs, and vanilla extract until the mixture is smooth and well-blended.

5. Add the wet ingredients to the dry mixture, stirring until the batter is well incorporated.

6. Pour the batter into a pair of 9-inch, non-stick, round cake pans. Lightly tap each pan on a counter to level the cake batter.

7. Bake for 30-35 minutes or until a toothpick inserted in the center comes out clean.

8. Take the pans out and let them cool for 10 minutes.

9. Carefully invert the cake layers onto racks and remove the pans.

10. Put the frosting ingredients, minus one of the two tablespoons of coconut oil, into a food processor and puree until smooth. Add the second tablespoon of coconut milk if needed. Place in the refrigerator until ready to use.

11. When the cake layers are completely cooled, apply frosting to the top surface of the bottom layer. Carefully set the top layer on top of the bottom layer and apply frosting to the top and sides of the second layer.

12. Slice and serve. Store the cake in the refrigerator until ready to serve, because the frosting might melt if it isn't kept cool.

No-bake Cheesecake (10)

This recipe is perfect for hot summer evenings when you don't feel like firing up the oven.

Servings: 8-12

Prep Time: 20 minutes

Cooking Time: 1 hour in the fridge

Ingredients for the Crust

- 2 cups raw mixed nuts
- 1 cup pitted dates
- 2 tablespoons water
- Pinch of sea salt

Ingredients for the Filling

- Meat from 2 Thai coconuts
- 2 cups macadamia nuts and/or cashews, soaked
- ¾ cup lemon juice
- ½ cup plus 1 tablespoon coconut butter
- 3 tablespoons coconut palm sugar
- 1 ¼ cup coconut water, held in reserve

Ingredients for the Topping

- 3 cups blueberries
- Splash of lemon juice
- 1 teaspoon coconut nectar

Directions

1. Put the nuts for the crust into a food processor and process until the nuts are almost a powder and they start sticking to the sides of the processor.

2. Add the dates and blend until the mixture starts to ball up. With the machine still running, start adding the coconut water. Stop when the clumps of mixture suddenly ball up in a solid mass.

3. Put the nut crust into a spring form pan, pressing the crust onto the bottom and up the sides.

4. Put all the ingredients for the filling into a blender in the order listed. Start the blender on low and increase the speed until the mixture is smooth and creamy.

5. Pour the filling mixture onto the crust and refrigerate until it sets, which takes an hour or more.

6. Put the ingredients for the topping into a small bowl. Mash them with a fork or a potato masher. You can leave some of the berries whole to improve the texture of the topping. Spoon some of the topping onto each individual slice of cheesecake.

Banana Cream Pie (10)

What's a recipe book without banana cream pie? This amazing recipe is absolutely delicious, yet it doesn't use any flour or dairy products. This makes a 9-inch pie.

Servings: 8 (pieces of pie)

Prep Time: 30 minutes

Cooking Time: 15 minutes

Total Time: 1 hour, 20 minutes (including fridge time)

Ingredients for the Crust

- 1 ½ cup almond flour (blanched preferred)
- ¼ teaspoon sea salt
- ¼ teaspoon ground cinnamon
- ¼ teaspoon baking soda
- ¼ cup coconut oil, melted
- 1 tablespoon filtered water

Ingredients for the Filling

- 2 cups raw cashews, soaked for 6-8 hours and then drained
- 2 medium ripe bananas
- 1/3 cup coconut oil, melted
- 1/3 cup honey
- 1 tablespoon vanilla extract

Ingredients for the Topping

- 1 can of full-fat, refrigerated coconut milk
- 2 tablespoons honey

- 1 teaspoon vanilla extract
- ½ banana, cut into slices (for garnishing)

Directions

1. Preheat your oven to 350 F. Grease a 9-inch pie plate.

2. In a large mixing bowl, combine the dry ingredients for the crust, mixing them well.

3. Add the coconut oil and water to the dry mix, blending until the flour mixture is worked into a dough. Press the dough into the bottom and sides of the pie pan evenly, patching any tears with dough.

4. Poke holes in the dough with a fork. Bake it for 10-15 minutes, until the edges of the crust are light golden brown. Put the pan on a wire rack to cool.

5. For the filling, combine the drained cashews, banana, honey and vanilla extract in a food processor or blender. Blend at low speed at first, but gradually increase the speed to high. Slowly add the coconut oil while continuing to blend, until the mixture is creamy and chunk-less.

6. Once the crust is completely cooled, pour the filling mixture into it. Place in the fridge for an hour or more, until it sets.

7. For the topping, first scoop out all the full-fat coconut cream from the top of the can (leaving the coconut water in the can) and put it into a mixing bowl. Add the honey and vanilla extract and beat with an electric hand mixer until the ingredients are well-mixed and the mixture attains the consistency of whipped cream.

8. Once the pie has set and you're ready to serve it, take it out of the fridge and spread the topping over it. Set the sliced bananas on top.

Chocolate Fudge Brownies (10)

Is there anything better than fudge brownies? And these brownies are even healthy.

Servings: 12-18 brownies

Prep Time: 15 minutes

Cooking Time: 25-30 minutes

Ingredients

- ½ cup coconut flour
- ½ cup raw cacao powder
- ½ cup raw honey
- 1/3 cup coconut oil, melted
- 5 eggs
- 2 tablespoons water
- ½ teaspoon salt
- ½ teaspoon baking soda

Directions

1. Preheat oven to 350 F. Grease an 8 x 8-inch baking dish, or line it with parchment paper.

2. Combine the dry ingredients and mix them well.

3. Combine the rest of the ingredients in a separate bowl. Mix them well.

4. Slowly stir the dry ingredients into the wet ones.

5. Pour the batter into the baking dish, smoothing the batter with a knife.

6. Bake for 25-30, testing with a toothpick inserted into the middle of the pan. When it comes out clean, the brownies are done.

7. Remove from the oven and let it cool for ten minutes, then cut into squares.

Conclusion

This book has provided an introduction to the Paleo Diet and its amazing ability to help people lose weight and improve their health. The Paleo Diet is the most natural diet possible, because it's the diet that humanity ate for millions of years before the introduction of agriculture.

This book offers fifty easy-to-follow Paleo recipes for shedding pounds and inches while contributing to your physical and mental wellbeing. These recipes are structured in a consistent format that provides the prep and cooking time for each recipe, as well as the number of servings. The directions are thorough, clear and concise. The dishes are varied, covered a broad base of foods, giving you a well-balanced selection of foods to choose from.

These fifty delicious Paleo recipes are just a start. Through them, you'll be able to better understand how you can substitute Paleo-friendly foods for many of the non-Paleo foods in your existing recipes from other sources. This expansion of your Paleo food choices can lead you and your family to not only trimmer figures, but also a fuller, healthier and happier life.

Helpful Resources

1. http://allrecipes.com/recipes/healthy-recipes/special-diets/paleo-diet/

2. http://paleoleap.com/paleo-diet-recipes/

3. http://www.elanaspantry.com/paleo-diet-recipes/

4. http://wellnessmama.com/2185/apple-cinnamon-coconut-flour-muffins/

5. http://thepaleodiet.com/recipes/

6. http://www.paleoplan.com/recipes/

7. *Paleo Diet Made Easy* by Scarlet Atkins

8. *40 Top Paleo Recipes* by Jenny Allan

9. *Green Smoothie Recipes for Weight Loss and Detox* by Jenny Allan

10. *Your Favorite Foods—Paleo Style! Part 2* by Angela Anottacelli

11. *100 Best Paleo Recipes* by Martha Stone

Preview of Gluten Free Diet Guide: A Blueprint to Jump Starting a Healthy, Low Budget, Gluten-Free Diet

Background

Gluten is a protein compound present in cereal grains such as wheat, rye and barley. Gluten is a Latin word which translates to "glue," referring to the combined water-insoluble proteins, gliadin and glutenin. Gluten is the substance that makes dough elastic and processed food items like bread, pasta and pastries chewy. This substance may also be present in cosmetics such as make-up and hair products.

A significant percentage of the population in North America have sensitivity to gluten where they experience an elevated immunologic response when they ingest foods that contain gluten. This usually leads to symptoms such as joint pain, anemia, tiredness, infertility, neurological disorders, dermatitis, and celiac disease, an autoimmune disorder.

The only known treatment for these health issues is to totally embrace a gluten-free diet. This means the person has to steer clear of foods that contain rye, barley, wheat, and other associated cereal grains. Because of the popularity of these grains in the food market, it is possible that items claiming to be gluten-free may have minute amounts of wheat, rye, or barley that is substantial enough to cause symptoms to persons that are sensitive to gluten.

Symptoms and disorders caused by gluten-containing food items

A review from the New England Journal of Medicine came up with a listing of illnesses caused by ingestion of gluten. Symptoms include Attention Deficit Hyperactivity Disorder (ADHD), anxiety, arthritis, depression, Irritable Bowel Syndrome (IBS), recurrent headaches, osteoporosis, eczema, fatigue, uncoordinated muscles, compromised immune system, inflammation of organs, excessive growth of fungus, weight loss or weight gain, and deficient nutrition. People who are hypersensitive to gluten are at high risk to develop diabetes, Gastro-Intestinal cancers, obesity, brain disorders, thyroid problems, and autism.

Costs involved with a gluten-free diet

A recent study assessed the economic burden of subscribing to a total gluten-free diet. The researchers conducted an analysis of food products that use wheat classified by brand name, size or weight of the package, and evaluated them in contrast to items that are gluten-free. The price disparities were also evaluated among different store venues like general stores, more expensive grocery stores, health food stores, and online grocery sites.

The study found that availability of gluten-free products varies among stores. General grocery stores offer 36 percent, while upper class grocery stores have 41 percent, and health food stores carry 94 percent in comparison to a hundred percent availability in online grocery sites. On the whole, all gluten-free products were costlier than wheat-based food items. Gluten-free pasta and bread are double the price of wheat-based pastas and breads.

Apparently, the purchase venue had more impact on the price ranges than geographic location. Researchers conclude that gluten-free items are not as available and are costlier than products that contain gluten. The author emphasizes that there is a need to address availability and cost issues of gluten-free foods that affect the dietary adherence and quality of life of gluten-sensitive consumers.

To fully enjoy this book, visit:

http://www.amazon.com/Gluten-Free-Diet-Guide-Blueprint-ebook/dp/B00I135OZO

Did You Like This Book?

Before you leave, I wanted to say thank you again for buying my book.

I know you could have picked from a number of different books on this topic, but you chose this one so I can't thank you enough for doing that and reading until the end.

I'd like to ask you a small favor.

If you enjoyed this book or feel that it has helped you in anyway, then could you please take a minute and post an honest review about it on Amazon?

Click here to post a review.

Your review will help get my book out there to more people and they'll be grateful, as will I.

More Books You Might Like

Household DIY: Save Time and Money with Do It Yourself Hints and Tips on Furniture, Clothes, Pests, Stains, Residues, Odors and More!

DIY Household Hacks: Save Time and Money with Do It Yourself Tips and Tricks for Cleaning Your House

Essential Oils: Essential Oils & Aromatherapy for Beginners: Proven Secrets to Weight Loss, Skin Care, Hair Care & Stress Relief Using Essential Oil Recipes

Apple Cider Vinegar for Beginners: An Apple Cider Vinegar Handbook with Proven Secrets to Natural Weight Loss, Optimum Health and Beautiful Skin

Body Butter Recipes: Proven Formula Secrets to Making All Natural Body Butters that Will Hydrate and Rejuvenate Your Skin

If the links do not work, for whatever reason, you can simply search for these titles on the Amazon website to find them.

Made in the USA
San Bernardino, CA
31 August 2015